FOREVER
SAFE

The Bible Answer To
Where Children Go
When They Die

DONALD STEWART

A book for parents who have suffered the loss of a young child.

Mt 18:14 Even so it is not the will of your Father which is in heaven, that one of these little ones should perish.

CONTENTS

FOREWORD
BY CARA PAGE

It has been a great privilege for me to have known Pastor Don Stewart for more than twenty years. He has been my pastor, my teacher, my counsellor and is a very, dear friend.

Pastor and Mrs. Stewart have experienced the grief of losing their little ones. They have been through those times of sorrow and brokenness which change a person forever. The comfort they received from the Lord and through his word is offered here in this book to others who may be experiencing this same sorrow and loss.

Even if you haven't lost a child, the message of FOREVER SAFE is for everyone. It explains the gospel of salvation found in the Lord Jesus Christ and the eternal life that is offered in Him. It challenges us as believers to guard this truth against all the false gospels and deceiving traditions which confront us at every turn. It exposes the lie of easy believism which replaces biblical repentance with saying a prayer. It explores why so many young people leave church and turn their backs on their Christian upbringing. It urges us as parents not to rush our children into making a profession of salvation in order to please us, but to keep our children's hearts that they may grow up in the knowledge and fear of God and one day come to genuine repentance and saving faith of their own.

No matter what loss or difficulty you may be facing, FOREVER SAFE will edify your faith, comfort your heart and remind you of the great truth that our God is a God of love. Your heart will be lifted from doubt in the midst of despair to hope and comfort through the promises of God's word.

ACKNOWLEDGEMENTS

Many thanks go to Cara Page for her support and tireless work and assistance in bringing this manuscript from an idea and burden to reality. As well as encouraging me to undertake such a task.

To my wife Luonna, for her help in proofing the text and daily encouragement.

To Tracy van Dijk, my secretary for her labour and help in putting words into print.

DEDICATION

The dedication of this book is to, first, my dear wife who went through the grief and pain of childbirth only to see the lifeless face of our little stillborn girl. Luonna has been a faithful servant of the Lord by my side for fifty years. Second to the memory of Dawn Joy, that little girl whose face I have never seen but finding hope and comfort through God's word I am assured we will meet one glad day in heaven. And, last of all to every parent who has endured the grief of the loss of a helpless child early in life. The promise of comfort from God's word is clear, they are FOREVER SAFE with our Lord. May the promises of God's word be your comfort.

CHAPTER ONE

THERE IS HOPE

And thou shalt be secure, because there is hope.
(Job 11:18)

One of the great questions of life stated in the book of Job has to do with life and death.

If a man die, shall he live again? (Job 14:14)

I want to be more specific and answer the question about children who die far too early. Many grieving parents ask, "Will we see our children again? What happens to these little ones when they die? What does the Bible say? Does God provide us with an answer? Is there hope to see our child again?"

This matter is a personal one for my wife and me. We have faced three miscarriages and have lost our little Dawn Joy six months into the pregnancy, who died strangling upon the cord. We understand the sorrow and heartache parents feel in such a situation. Because it is so personal for us, I have made it a matter of much study and prayer. I have desired to be able to provide others with comfort and hope from the scriptures, a hope that such little ones are forever safe in heaven with the Lord.

Just as in the book of Job, we find many of the questions in life hard to answer and equally hard to accept. As adults, we find any death hard to accept. However, when it comes to the matter of children, we see the death of a child more perplexing, even to the point that we may question God. These times require an answer from the word of God, which can bring comfort, peace and hope to those parents who know the Lord. There is hope and comfort for those parents who need the hope provided in scripture.

When we lost our little Dawn Joy, we were not prepared for it, and no one seemed to be able to give us solid answers of much-needed comfort and hope. Many years later, as a young Assistant Pastor, one of the young men in our church had a sister whose baby died of sudden infant death syndrome. My Pastor asked if I would be willing to officiate the graveside service. Admittedly, I panicked, wondering, what do I tell these people? How do I comfort these people? My heart went out to them because I knew their sorrow, yet I also knew that I struggled to find an honest answer of hope for them. At the ceremony, I concluded the service with a simple little poem that I found saying, "and baby sleeps." I walked away, knowing that a bit of poetry provided no real hope as sweet as it sounded.

I wanted answers, which led me to many years of study to find solid, biblical answers about where these little ones spend eternity. As one not wanting to give way to emotional and sentimental answers, my prayer has always been, Lord, please give me an answer from your word that I might give to others who need comfort and reassurance in such a tough time in their life.

The most popular answer in the Bible relates to David, who lost his infant son at an early age. After much prayer and fasting, his response was:

But now he is dead, wherefore should I fast? can I bring
him back again? I shall go to him, but he shall not return
to me.

(2 Samuel 12:23)

It is a remarkable passage, and the truth is plainly stated, "I shall
go to him," but I wanted to know if other scriptures were confirming this
comforting truth. Through the pages of this book, we will search the
scriptures for a more conclusive and satisfying answer.

While there are many scriptures regarding this topic, there are also
many conjectures. Many are false theories with no scriptural support,
and some are even contrary to scripture, and they are at most just ideas.
We aim to reprove these false theories and provide answers with a sound
scriptural basis and support.

Let us put some guidelines to our discussion, which will help us
find hope. Our question concerns children explicitly. We need to look
closely at the words used in scripture that define and describe children.
Can we place a particular age at which someone is still is a child? Does
scripture provide a set period at which any one child is accountable for
their actions, sometimes referred to as the age of accountability? Are we
saying that all children have the same intellectual capacity at a particular
age? The question becomes even more expansive as we think of intellectually challenged people to the degree that they cannot discern between
right and wrong, good and evil. Where will these spend eternity?

Consider the use of the word babe:

And it came to pass, that, when Elisabeth heard the saluta-
tion of Mary, the babe leaped in her womb; and Elisabeth
was filled with the Holy Ghost. (Luke 1:41)

To be taxed with Mary his espoused wife, being great with
child. (Luke 2:5)

And this shall be a sign unto you; Ye shall find the babe wrapped in swaddling clothes, lying in a manger. (Luke 2:12)

And they came with haste, and found Mary, and Joseph, and the babe lying in a manger. (Luke 2:16)

And when they were come into the house, they saw the young child with Mary his mother. (Matthew 2:11)

The Bible uses different words when describing children. It speaks of a child, a little child, or little ones. We can think of a babe, an infant, or even an unborn child. We all ask, at what age does one of these little ones, these babes come to know and understand the gospel and be saved? What happens if a child dies before this age is reached? It is interesting that in the book of Matthew, he starts with children, and in the same chapter and the same discussion, he goes from talking of a child to little children and then also uses the phrase, little ones. We are expressly told that it is not the Lord's will that any of these little ones perish. A couple of other verses help us understand this. In Matthew chapter 18, we read:

At the same time came the disciples unto Jesus, saying, Who is the greatest in the kingdom of heaven?

And Jesus called a little child unto him, and set him in the midst of them,

And said, Verily I say unto you, Except ye be converted, and become as little children, ye shall not enter into the kingdom of heaven.

Whosoever therefore shall humble himself as this little child, the same is greatest in the kingdom of heaven. (Matthew 18:1-4)

The Bible tells us that these little ones are precious to the Lord, and we are carefully warned to despise not even one of them:

> Take heed that ye despise not one of these little ones; for I say unto you, That in heaven their angels do always behold the face of my Father which is in heaven. (Matthew 18:10)

> Even so it is not the will of your Father which is in heaven, that one of these little ones should perish. (Matthew 18:14)

We find the use of "little ones" in the Old Testament as well as in the New Testament. Here in the book of Numbers, we read:

> But your little ones, which ye said should be a prey, them will I bring in, and they shall know the land which ye have despised. (Numbers 14:31)

It is talking specifically about those who would go through into the land of Canaan. We learn that all but two of the adults did not enter the promised land because of their unbelief. They sinned, knowingly ignoring God and his promises and fell short of trusting God. Yet their little ones were brought into the promised land.

How does the Bible define a little one? According to Strong's dictionary, as it is used here, the definition of a little one is one who trips at his gait, which means one who has just barely learned how to walk. The little ones were yet too young to believe or not to believe; these were preserved and brought safely into the promised land of Canaan.

Consider the actual numbers of the multitudes of little ones in our world today who leave us by death far too early. According to www. worldometers.info and the WHO, there are 125,000 abortions every day, equating to 40 – 50 million abortions per year. Where will these little ones spend eternity? One out of every 72 births is stillborn; that is one every

16 seconds. Where will they spend eternity? Job calls these **"an hidden untimely birth... infants which never saw light"** (Job 3:16).

What about SIDS, (Sudden Infant Death Syndrome)? It has been recorded that 19% of adults have experienced the death of a child. Is there hope for the parent of these children who has died? What about the intellectually challenged; are they not in the same category? There are 6 million people with down syndrome that is one in seven hundred babies globally. Where will all of these spend eternity? Other statistics claim that 29,000 children under the age of five die every day, 21 every minute.

According to scripture, salvation is a personal choice. What then happens to those who are too young to make an intelligent choice? They cannot talk, they cannot even walk, and they have no discernment between right and wrong. Will they be forever separated from God? The answer is a resounding no; they will be FOREVER SAFE with God.

As another principle of Bible study, let us look at three words: sleep, die, and perish and their definition and usage in scripture. Consider I Thessalonians 4, where the Bible gives an account to provide hope to people of God who had lost a loved one:

> **But I would not have you to be ignorant, brethren, concerning them which are asleep, that ye sorrow not, even as others which have no hope.**
>
> **For if we believe that Jesus died and rose again, even so them also which sleep in Jesus will God bring with him.**
>
> **For this we say unto you by the word of the Lord, that we which are alive and remain unto the coming of the Lord shall not prevent them which are asleep.**
>
> **For the Lord himself shall descend from heaven with a shout, with the voice of the archangel, and with the trump of God: and the dead in Christ shall rise first:**

Then we which are alive and remain shall be caught up
together with them in the clouds, to meet the Lord in the
air: and so shall we ever be with the Lord.

Wherefore comfort one another with these words.
(1Thessalonians 4:13-18)

It is interesting to note that the words die or perish were not used
here instead, the term sleep was used. What is the distinction between
the words die, perish and sleep? Why was the word sleep used concerning those who had died? To whom did the "no hope" apply? It was to
those who had never come to know Christ as Saviour in their lifetime.
Remember, he was offering hope to the saved regarding those who had
fallen asleep through death. Part of the answer lies in the use of the word
sleep. When one goes to sleep, we expect to wake up after a while and
continue on. Thus, he said, "Comfort one another with these words." The
scriptures provide us with a hope that gives us comfort in times of sorrow.
It is a hope not based on feeling, sentiment or emotion but rather upon
the unfailing word of God.

For whatsoever things were written aforetime were written
for our learning, that we through patience and comfort of
the scriptures might have hope. (Romans 15:4)

It is excellent to know that God is known in scripture and by experience as the God of all comfort.

Blessed be God, even the Father of our Lord Jesus Christ, the
Father of mercies, and the God of all comfort. (2 Corinthians 1:3)

Consider what the Bible says of the wicked, those who never have
been saved.

When a wicked man dieth, his expectation shall perish: and
the hope of unjust men perisheth. (Proverbs 11:7)

The Bible gives the wicked no hope when they die but further states that their expectation shall perish. In contrast, it is not God's will that these little ones perish:

Even so it is not the will of your Father which is in heaven, that one of these little ones should perish. (Matthew 18:14)

Neither is it God's will that any perish, but all should be saved. Peter writes:

The Lord is not slack concerning his promise, as some men count slackness; but is longsuffering to us-ward, not willing that any should perish, but that all should come to repentance. (2 Peter 3:9)

Little children do not understand right and wrong, good and evil and do not know repentance. Can a child that cannot even walk or talk come to repentance? The answer once again is a resounding no. In Chapter 2 of second Peter says:

But these, as natural brute beasts, made to be taken and destroyed, speak evil of the things that they understand not; and shall utterly perish in their own corruption. (2 Peter 2:12)

Why do some perish? It is because they sin. They die and perish in their corruption and sin. They openly rebel against God and reject him and his words. They then face the consequences of their sin, which is death. This death is eternal separation from God. However, all who have trusted Christ and are with him in heaven, have not and will not perish.

Websters 1828 dictionary defines the word perish as following:

1. To suffer divine wrath and punishment in the future world.

2. To be lost eternally, to suffer eternal misery.

Do you think God will allow these little ones to suffer divine wrath? Will they face eternal damnation and perish? No, God is not willing that they perish. They are, in fact, safe for all of eternity because of our loving God.

Consider the use of the words die and death used here in Ezekiel:

> **The soul that sinneth, it shall die. The son shall not bear the iniquity of the Father, neither shall the Father bear the iniquity of the son: the righteousness of the righteous shall be upon him, and the wickedness of the wicked shall be upon him. (Ezekiel 18:20)**

The Bible clearly states that "the soul that sinneth" shall die. It is a biblical truth that everyone is born with a sinful nature, including children.

> **For all have sinned, and come short of the glory of God; (Romans 3:23)**

This sin nature is the source of our sin. The soul that sinned refers to a personal action of transgressing the word of God. Does a little child know what sin is and that sin is a transgression of the law of God?

The term die in the Bible is used in two ways. One is of physical death as used here in the book of Hebrews:

> **And as it is appointed unto men once to die, but after this the judgment. (Hebrew 9:27)**

There is also a second death for those who die without Christ. That death is eternal separation from God. A judgment for their sin. Those who die unsaved perish, facing God's judgment due to their sin. The book of Romans states:

> **For the wages of sin is death; but the gift of God is eternal life through Jesus Christ our Lord. (Romans 6:23)**

Has the little child sinned against God knowingly, willingly, and rebelliously? No, it has not.

In John chapter 11, we find the Lord using the word sleep for death:

These things said he: and after that he saith unto them, Our friend Lazarus sleepeth; but I go, that I may awake him out of sleep.

Then said his disciples, Lord, if he sleep, he shall do well.

Howbeit Jesus spake of his death: but they thought that he had spoken of taking of rest in sleep.

Then said Jesus unto them plainly, Lazarus is dead. (John 11:11-14)

Lazarus had died. The disciples wanted Jesus to do something, and Jesus told them that Lazarus was sleeping. The disciples thought of sleep as going to bed for the night. They thought, well if he is asleep and not dead as reported, there is nothing to worry about. Jesus then clarified it so that they understood, using the term dead. Later Jesus spoke with a promise stating that whoever believes in him shall never die:

And whosoever liveth and believeth in me shall never die. Believest thou this? (John 11:26)

We see why he said he was asleep. It is said of the child of God that those who have died are asleep, not dead or perished. We thus have a sure hope that those who know the Lord are saved and will not perish and those who are yet too young to understand salvation are safe, having never known sin and its consequences.

Read what our Lord Jesus said in Luke chapter 18:

And they brought unto him also infants, that he would touch them: but when his disciples saw it, they rebuked them.

But Jesus called them unto him, and said, Suffer little children to come unto me, and forbid them not: for of such is the kingdom of God. (Luke 18:15-16)

Note here that Jesus referred to infants and little children as those who would inherit the kingdom of God. It is not his will that any of these little ones should perish. Those who die prematurely will be in the kingdom of God. We who are saved will see them again.

There is hope. Scripture abounds in the clear teaching that little ones are innocent. They are loved and watched over by their heavenly Father and will be FOREVER SAFE with Him when they die. This truth brings excellent comfort and hope. It exalts the greatness of God's love and kindness and the depth of his justice and holiness.

"Great and marvellous are thy works, Lord God Almighty; just and true are thy ways, thou King of saints" (Revelation 15:3).

CHAPTER TWO
THESE LITTLE ONES

**Even so it is not the will of your Father which is in heaven that
one of these little ones should perish.**

(Matthew 18:14)

A s Christians, we want to be able to say yes; little children will go to
be with the Lord when they die. We need to have a secure understanding of this doctrine based on scripture to correct false teachings and
provide biblical assurance. In this chapter, we will examine some false theories and contrast them with the true teaching of the word of God.

What is a theory? What is a hypothesis? According to Webster's
Dictionary, a theory refers to speculation. A hypothesis is an assumed
proposition. Both can be vague and unsubstantiated. They refer to what
you believe, expect, and presume about an issue that may or may not be
correct, a conjecture without firm evidence, or a belief without substanti-
ating proof. For instance, I think and speculate that this is what happened
or that this will happen. It's vague and provides no real assurance. It may
even be the opposite of factual evidence and biblical truth.

Let's consider four false theories which are put forward with
regards to where little children go when they die:

1. The idea that children become angels when they die.

2. The assumption that the age of accountability is twelve years old.

3. The false assurance that infant baptism saves children.

4. The unfounded belief in household salvation.

Not long after I came to Australia, as Pastor of Emmanuel Independent Baptist Church, we had a relatively large youth group. One of the young girls called me one night and said, "I need you to go and visit my mother and father in the hospital; they want you to come quickly." I asked why. She said, "Well, mom has delivered a baby, and it has died. They want you to come straight away and baptize the baby." So, I thought, all the way there, what am I going to say to them? What am I going to face when I get there? Having been through that personally with my wife in the death of our baby; I prayed, Lord, give me some wisdom to know what to say.

As I walked into the room, their infant child's lifeless little body lay inside a crib. The father and mother were heartbroken, utterly devastated. They asked me imploringly, with tears in their eyes, "What are we going to do?" I looked at them while quietly praying, Lord, please help me. A nurse walked in with a silver pan filled with water. She said, "Here, you might need this." The parents informed me that this was needed so that I could baptise their baby for them.

You talk about getting caught in a tricky situation. A broken-hearted mom and a dad in tears are next to their newborn's, lifeless body. Their hopes and dreams for this little child's life are in tatters. Their plans and expectations for their new family member lie in pieces. They think that if I baptise this child, it will be saved. They will be comforted with false hope. Their grief will be satisfied. I thanked the nurse and politely explained that we would not need the bowl of water.

What a challenging time that was. Tears streamed down the face of the distraught parents, looking to me to provide some hope to their shattered lives. I said, "I know what you want, but I am saying to you that there is hope in scripture that a little child like this one laying over here, when they die, will go to be with the Lord. There is no need to baptise them." I did not go into all the other doctrinal reasons to say that it is a false doctrine, but I wanted to say that there is another hope, an honest and trustworthy hope based upon the word of God. These are real-life experiences, and to be there and provide an accurate and comforting answer is tricky. From those times onward, this issue has been a burden on my heart. My prayer has been, Lord, to show me more concrete answers from your word to be able to give hope to people when faced with this kind of loss.

Please consider the first false theory: children become angels when they die. I hear people with a newborn babe looking down and saying, "Isn't it such a little angel?" And I say, "Give it time". Talk to me in two years and see if that little one still is the little angel that it is now." Those are sweet and endearing words but give it time. The real question, is whether or not children become angels when they die? What does the bible tell us about angels? Can we, from scripture, distinguish between angels and children? In the book of Hebrews, we read:

Are they not all ministering *spirits*, sent forth to minister for them who shall be heirs of salvation? (Hebrews 1:14)

We could use many verses, but I am going to highlight just a few and make some statements. Take notice of the word "spirits". Angels are created beings. God creates them. They are spirit beings, not human beings.

We moved to Evanston, Wyoming, to start a church. We lived outside of town in a trailer home. The family across the unit from us had an infant child that died. We wanted to show our sympathy to them and so we went to the graveside service. They were of a different religious persuasion, and I did not know what to expect. As we were out there on that cold snowy day, I first noticed that the man who officiated the service had not even met the family and had to introduce himself at the service. I listened to him, as often happens when I go to funerals and hear false doctrine, I find it challenging to sit through. I listened to this man state that the little one had been a spirit wandering in the heavens until he was born and that God now needed this little spirit back. I thought to myself, there is no scriptural support for what you just said. Can you not give this family any more hope than nonsense like that?

I am saying these things as they hit hard in my heart. We need to give sound Biblical answers. I was searching for more answers myself. It was not that I doubted God; I wanted to give a more biblical foundation for the answers to the questions which perplexed me. Little children were not spirits before they were born. "**Children are a heritage of the LORD" (Psalm 127:3)**. Angels are spirit beings created by God. Angels are spirit beings without a body. There are a lot of ideas about angels, such as angels have wings, angels play the harps, and angels have halos around their heads. We need to stop looking at how the world pictures angels; stop listening to conjecture concerning children and angels. These are deceptive and misleading. Our understanding of them must be based entirely upon the word of God as the final authority.

If you would, I want you to go with me to Matthew 22:30, which gives us a deeper insight into this matter. There are many other verses, but we are taking a brief look here at what the Bible says about angels:

> **For in the resurrection they neither marry, nor are given in marriage, but are as the angels of God in heaven. (Matthew 22:30)**

Pay close attention to where it says, **"nor are given in marriage, but are as the angels of God in heaven."** We tend to assume that angels have gender. That is hard to prove. While angels are revealed in many different forms in scripture, we understand that angels do not procreate. Angels do not have angels. There was a set, limited number of angels at creation. Some of those rebelled against God and these God "**hath reserved in everlasting chains under darkness unto the judgment of the great day**" (Jude 7).

Again, angels are spirit beings. They appear in different forms. They can appear as people, and we might not even know it. "**Be not forgetful to entertain strangers:**" the bible says, "**for thereby some have entertained angels unawares.**" (**Hebrews 13:2**). The question we are seeking to answer is, do children become angels? Notice again, "**but are *as* the angels of God.**" We do not become angels but are as angels. Our resurrected bodies will, in some ways, be like the angels, but in heaven, we are still intrinsically separate beings from angels. We need to stop and realise that children are a part of the kingdom of God, "**for such is the kingdom of heaven.**" We see that children becoming angels when they die is not a biblical truth. It is a false theory.

Next, let us consider the question regarding the supposed age of accountability? At what age, if there is a specific age, does a child get to where they can know and discern between good and evil? At what age do they have the discernment to see the difference between good and evil? Does the Bible give us an age? Is it 8, is it 10, is it 5, or is it 7? Sometimes people ask me, "Is my child old enough to be saved?" I say, "I cannot answer that question. I can tell you that every child today is not of the same intellectual capacity even though they might be of the same age."

And that, in and of itself, begins to answer our question. We talk about the *age* of accountability; from a Biblical standpoint, we are not talking about a period from 9 to 10 or 11 or 12. We are talking about an understanding or a level of intellectual maturity. Some think that at 12, they get to that place of understanding. But I would say that if they are brought up in a Christian household, they will learn about spiritual things more quickly than others. A parent may teach them early in life. But what if they are brought up in a home that does not know of God. It may be a long time, if ever, that they come to that standpoint of knowing good and evil.

Accountability is the keyword because accountability refers to the age at which they become personally responsible for their sin. We know the Bible teaches us that every child is born with a sinful nature. But as a little one, he does not sin knowingly. He does not openly say, "I know that's the word of God, but I'm going to reject that." Does a one-year-old do that? No. Does a 2-year-old do that? No. At what age does a child begin to do that? I cannot tell you. So, who does know? Only God. Only God can know for sure. I got saved at the age of 7. I know that my sister got saved at 5. Some do not understand till 9 or 10, and maybe not even then. The knowledge of good and evil, my friends, is the key to answering this whole question about FOREVER SAFE.

We read further in the book of Psalms, chapter 106:

> Yea, they sacrificed their sons and their daughters unto devils,
>
> And shed innocent blood, even the blood of their sons and of their daughters, whom they sacrificed unto the idols of Canaan: and the land was polluted with blood. (Psalm 106:37-38)

This takes us back to earlier in Old Testament times of the nation of Israel when they sacrificed their sons and their daughters to a god they called Molech. Verse 38 speaks of innocent blood; the keyword is innocent. God declared these children whom they sacrificed were innocent. Is that child, born with a sinful nature, still innocent? Does he know what sin is? Does he know that sin is a transgression of the law of God? Does he know that he has sinned against God? I would say "No".

The word innocent is a legal term used in a court of law. Innocent means that they are exempt and without guilt. I am saying to you that when we look at the age of accountability regarding those children who die before this age, whatever age it is, they are still innocent. They are not guilty before God; they are not guilty before the law because they do not even understand the knowledge of good and evil.

God, we know, is not willing that any one of these little ones should perish. Scripture clarifies that children are not angels, but Jesus said, **"their angels do always behold the face of my Father which is in heaven" (Matthew 18:10).** The bible tells us that the murder of little children is the shedding of innocent blood and that **"whosoever shall offend one of these little ones that believe in me, it is better for him that a millstone were hanged about his neck, and he were cast into the sea" (Mark 9:42).**

There comes an age when we all become accountable before God for our sins. We call it the age of accountability. That age is relative to each person, and only God in heaven knows when someone has reached that age. Until that stage, we can know and rest assured that these little ones are loved by our Lord, guarded by angels and forever safe in the eternal kingdom of our heavenly Father.

CHAPTER THREE
IN HIS ARMS

**And he took them up in his arms, put his hands upon them,
and blessed them.**

(Mark 10:16)

False theories about life after death abound. Any hope built upon a false theory and a false gospel will fail you. We want to provide true hope from the scriptures and clear up false hope and false theories. One of the largest false teachings in the world today concerns infant baptism. I want to point out some reasons why it's not acceptable and to show you how you can help others to come to a sound understanding of the truth in this matter.

We mentioned in the previous chapter about one of the more difficult times I've had in the ministry was when I was called late one night to go to a hospital and help a family whose child was stillborn. The baby was laying there lifeless, and the nurse walked in with the pan of water that I might use to sprinkle a few drops over the stillborn child. How sad. Sometimes you get caught in situations that are very difficult and extremely emotional. As Christians, we're not to be ruled by emotions. We're to be ruled by the word of God. Many would have thought to just go ahead and sprinkle the water over that lifeless child, justifying it in terms of having provided comfort to the grieving parents. It would only have provided them with false hope and a corrupt understanding of the gospel.

In Mark chapter 10 we read:

> **And they brought young children to him, that he should touch them: and his disciples rebuked those that brought them.**
>
> **But when Jesus saw it, he was much displeased, and said unto them, Suffer the little children to come unto me, and forbid them not: for of such is the kingdom of God.**
>
> **Verily I say unto you, Whosoever shall not receive the kingdom of God as a little child, he shall not enter therein.**
>
> **And he took them up in his arms, put his hands upon them, and blessed them. (Mark 10:13-16)**

Notice what takes place, if you would. They brought young children to him that he should touch them, and his disciples rebuked those that brought them. They, unfortunately, saw the children as a nuisance and tried to send them away. When Jesus saw it, the Bible tells us, he was much displeased. He said to them, **"Suffer the little children to come unto me, and forbid them not: for of such is the kingdom of God"** (**Mark 10:14**). I'm assuming here that it's a parent who has understood who this miracle worker is, who this Jesus is and what he can do and so they brought their children to him. They have a legitimate concern. They want the Lord's blessing on their children. They want their children to be secure not only in this life but also in the life to come.

What type of people are in the kingdom of God? Saved people who have come to know the Lord Jesus Christ having realized that they are a sinner and asked for the forgiveness of sins repented and now are truly saved. But what about these little children? What about the aborted? What about the stillborn? What about those who died of SIDS? What about the disabled, those who are intellectually challenged with regard to their ability to understand? God is not willing, the Lord Jesus Christ is not willing, that any should perish. What was Jesus' response in this situation? He blessed them. Why did he do that? Because our God is one that loves. Our Lord is one of compassion. He blessed them as a way of expressing his love and concern for them.

I also want you to notice what Jesus did not do. He did not instruct them to take those children and baptize them. In fact, Jesus' baptism was as an adult, not a child. He did not tell the disciples to sprinkle them with water. He did not give them any instruction on that whatsoever. Instead, he blessed them. He took them up in his arms and touched them and blessed them.

In Matthew chapter 18, Jesus said:

> **But whoso shall offend one of these little ones which** *believe* *in* **me, it were better for him that a millstone were hanged about his neck, and that he were drowned in the depth of the sea. (Matthew 18:6)**

When you ask a little child what they believe in, you'll find they believe in a lot of things. But we understand as adults that there is a difference between believing "in" and believing "on" when it comes to salvation. Believing in Jesus is different from believing on the work he did for us. It is interesting the words that Jesus used when he spoke of the matter of belief and believing in. You can believe in the Lord Jesus Christ and not be saved. The Bible tells us, "**The devils also believe, and tremble**" (**James 2:19**). I might believe in a person and yet not believe in or on what they do.

What then does it mean to believe? Believing on has to do with salvation and the fact that we are sinners, and we need to repent of our sins and ask the Lord Jesus Christ to forgive us of our sins. It means believing on his work and not my own for salvation. A one-year-old does not understand that. A two-year-old does not understand that. In fact, we do not know at what specific age they understand the gospel truth.

You could write a whole book on the errors of infant baptism. There are many who have taken that infant child, that small child, that one-week-old child and they have had somebody sprinkle water over him with the belief that the child is now saved and going to heaven. Most of the people who take their child to be christened and consequently baptized, do so out of concern. I appreciate that concern. But we certainly do not want them to have false hope. They will take them with the idea that when this child is sprinkled with water that they are now saved. And I would say to you, the child had no choice in the matter whatsoever. None at all. This sprinkling provides false hope and comfort for the parents. It does absolutely nothing good to or for the child. Instead, it brings confusion and misunderstanding. It teaches a false gospel of works and causes untold spiritual damage for its false and deceptive hope.

We want to eliminate false hope and provide a scriptural hope throughout this context. We witness to children who are 9, 10, and 11 years old, and the parents may not be saved, and the child goes home and is excited that he is saved and says, "I'm going to get baptized." The parents say, "Oh no, you were baptized when you were a child." Too often we have seen this happen. In fact, they refuse to let that child get baptized because they were sprinkled as an infant. They did this with the false understanding that baptism will provide salvation and eternal life in heaven. This causes confusion and doubts for the child regarding when his salvation really took place and blocks his need to obey the Lord in getting scripturally baptized.

What does the Bible say? Salvation, according to the word of God, is a free choice. We need to understand that. Can the stillborn make a choice? They had no opportunity for a choice. What choice can the aborted have? None. Can little children understand what it means to sin against God? They are too young to be able to make that free choice to get saved.

I will ask you a question. It's an obvious question but it bears asking. Was Jesus an infant when he got baptized? No. Was he a child when he got baptized? No. Is Jesus supposed to be our example of what to do? Yes. When Jesus was baptized, was he sprinkled? No. Well, let's ask the question why not? And why was Jesus baptized? Mary, the Lord's mother, went on to claim that Jesus was her saviour. I would submit to you, and you know this, Jesus was not baptized because he needed to be forgiven of his sin. He was the one without sin. What hope did his baptism provide? What does it show us? When was he baptized? How was he baptized? Did they sprinkle a little bit of water over the top of him and say, "Now you're baptized"? No, he went down into the water and came back up out of the water, and he is our example.

When they brought the little children to Jesus, I ask the question, why didn't Jesus tell them, "Go and have this child baptized"? Why didn't he, in his rebuke of the disciples, give the instruction of what that child needed? Instead, he took the little children into his arms and blessed them and said, "For of such is the kingdom of God." The little ones believed in him. The bible instructs us to have childlike faith and childlike innocence. But never does it instruct us to baptize infants.

In the book of Acts, we read:

And the eunuch answered Philip, and said, I pray thee, of whom speaketh the prophet this? of himself, or of some other man?

Then Philip opened his mouth, and began at the same scripture, and preached unto him Jesus.

27

And as they went on their way, they came unto a certain water: and the eunuch said, See, here is water; what doth hinder me to be baptized?

And Philip said, If thou believest with all thine heart, thou mayest. And he answered and said, I believe that Jesus Christ is the Son of God.

And he commanded the chariot to stand still: and they went down both into the water, both Philip and the eunuch; and he baptized him.

And when they were come up out of the water, the Spirit of the Lord caught away Philip, that the eunuch saw him no more: and he went on his way rejoicing. (Acts 8:34-39)

This is the account of Philip and the eunuch. The eunuch was reading from the word of God, and he didn't understand what he was reading; Philip spoke to him and witnessed to him at that point. Then the eunuch asked the question, "Is there any reason why I can't get baptized?" Philip has just preached to him Jesus and the eunuch is thinking in terms of baptism and with all this water, he wants to get baptized. "Is there any reason why I shouldn't get baptized?" he asks.

In verse 37, Philip gives a prerequisite for baptism:

And Philip said, If thou believest with all thine heart, thou mayest. And he answered and said, I believe that Jesus Christ is the Son of God. (Acts 8:37)

This is a matter of salvation. He preached unto him, Jesus. When he said, "I want to get baptized," Philip said, "No, no sense you getting baptized until you get saved." I'm putting it in our vernacular. I ask you the question, why are people baptizing little children when the biblical instruction is you must first believe on the Lord Jesus Christ and believe with all of your heart? You do not need to get baptized prior to that because all you will get is wet.

Let's go one step farther. In verses 38 and 39 we read:

> And he commanded the chariot to stand still: and they went *down both into the water*, both Philip and the eunuch; and he baptized him.
>
> And when they were come *up out of the water*, the Spirit of the Lord caught away Philip, that the eunuch saw him no more: and he went on his way rejoicing. (Acts 8:38-39)

Notice the two phrases, "down into the water" and "up out of the water." He wasn't sprinkled, my friends. He came up out of the water. We understand from this that baptism is by immersion. So, we look at the biblical account and we see that it is contrary to what is practised in many churches today.

I would submit to you this, there is not one place in scripture where you will find that a child is baptized. Not one. I challenge people to show it to me. In fact, if we are going to take the examples of scripture, it was always adults who had believed on the Lord Jesus Christ, regarding salvation who then got baptized. When we study scripture, we do not find infant baptism to be a biblical practice. It is just not there. In fact, it is completely contrary to scripture. The very belief, reason and mode of infant baptism are all contrary to what the bible teaches.

Why then do we have infant baptism? That doesn't take too long to figure out. I'm not going to take a seven-week-old child and dunk it underneath the water. This is about convenience and altering the word of God to meet that convenience. The tragedy is this, my friends, people believe these things and it's a false hope. It's false security. It's a false gospel. For those parents who think that their child got saved when it was baptized, they will have no need to see them saved for the rest of their lives. It effectively closes a door in that child's life to the true gospel and their unmet and yet unfulfilled need for salvation.

This leads us to another false theory and that is the idea of household salvation. Some people put it this way. God has no grandchildren. I put it to you like this, salvation is not by proxy. You cannot pray for somebody else to be saved and then they'll be forgiven, because of your prayer, so to speak. It has to be something personal between them and the Lord. I can pray for you to get saved and I can only hope that you would get saved but my prayer doesn't save you. It's your personal decision. But what about those who cannot even make that decision, they're not that far along, and who don't have the mental capacity?

Look at Acts chapter 16:

And a certain woman named Lydia, a seller of purple, of the city of Thyatira, which worshipped God, heard us: whose heart the Lord opened, that she attended unto the things which were spoken of Paul.

And when she was baptized, and her household, she besought us, saying, If ye have judged me to be faithful to the Lord, come into my house, and abide there. And she constrained us. (Acts 16:14-15)

Notice in verse 14 the phrase, "whose heart the Lord opened." Some people take this verse and speak of it in the context of household salvation. We're talking about the salvation of Lydia. We find out that it was a matter of the Lord opening her heart unto salvation and when it says she was baptized and her household, you cannot take that and declare that this has to do with infant salvation because it nowhere says how old they in her household were. We cannot argue from the silence of scripture. There's no justifiable argument here. What we are told is that after they had witnessed to Lydia and her heart was opened, and she received the Lord and was saved, she was then baptized. Those in her household who also heard and understood the gospel and received the Lord were likewise baptized. This is the consistent pattern of scripture.

In the same chapter, we read of the Philippian jailer and his salvation and then subsequent baptism. It tells us:

> And at midnight Paul and Silas prayed, and sang praises unto God: and the prisoners heard them.
>
> And suddenly there was a great earthquake, so that the foundations of the prison were shaken: and immediately all the doors were opened, and every one's bands were loosed.
>
> And the keeper of the prison awaking out of his sleep, and seeing the prison doors open, he drew out his sword, and would have killed himself, supposing that the prisoners had been fled.
>
> But Paul cried with a loud voice, saying, Do thyself no harm: for we are all here.
>
> Then he called for a light, and sprang in, and came trembling, and fell down before Paul and Silas,
>
> And brought them out, and said, Sirs, what must I do to be saved?
>
> And they said, Believe on the Lord Jesus Christ, and thou shalt be saved, and thy house.
>
> And they spake unto him the word of the Lord, and to all that were in his house.
>
> And he took them the same hour of the night, and washed their stripes; and was baptized, he and all his, straightway.
>
> (Acts 16:25-33)

Notice in Verse 30 how he asks, "Sirs, what must I do to be saved?" That's the question. Remember the eunuch said, "What doth hinder me to be baptized?" We come back to verse 31, "Believe on the Lord Jesus Christ, and thou shalt be saved, and thy house."

So again, there are those who want to talk about household salvation and if you get saved your children are automatically included, but that's not what it's saying here. It's definitely not talking about anything to do with infant baptism. We need to realize that baptism comes after salvation. We cannot put things into scripture that are not there. We come back to the matter of salvation and the instruction to "believe on the Lord Jesus Christ," which is stated in verse 31, and then followed by baptism in verse 33.

The biblical order is always belief, salvation and then baptism. The false understanding of household salvation takes away from the clear and consistent teaching of scripture that salvation is a personal choice.

Parents have a profound influence on their children, but they cannot force them to get saved. Each person must make that decision for themselves of their own free will and with their own understanding. Salvation is a personal choice and with infant baptism, and the belief in household salvation, the child has no choice whatsoever. Ezekiel chapter 18 explains it:

> **The soul that sinneth, it shall die. The son shall not bear the iniquity of the father, neither shall the father bear the iniquity of the son: the righteousness of the righteous shall be upon him, and the wickedness of the wicked shall be upon him. (Ezekiel 18:20)**

Every little child is born with a sin nature but has not yet sinned knowingly and willingly. They are innocent. They are forever safe. We can be comforted to know that the Lord, as busy as he was ministering to the needs of so many people, took the time to take these little ones into his arms and bless them. Our Lord cares for those who are small and weak and innocent. His word assures us that when they die, they will be found in the kingdom of God and safe in his loving arms.

CHAPTER 4

IS GOD FAIR?

**The LORD is righteous in all his ways,
and holy in all his works.
(Psalm 145:17)**

You may, and I hope that will be the case, never have to experience the sorrow of losing an infant child through SIDS, or through illness or through accident. You may certainly encounter someone who has suffered the loss of a child and is grieving. We want to be able to provide hope from the scriptures. The passage concerning David and his little son is the one that is most often given as proof of hope for a parent who has lost an infant child. We read in second Samuel the full account. It tells us:

> **And David said unto Nathan, I have sinned against the LORD. And Nathan said unto David, The LORD also hath put away thy sin; thou shalt not die.**
>
> **Howbeit, because by this deed thou hast given great occasion to the enemies of the LORD to blaspheme, the child also that is born unto thee shall surely die.**

And Nathan departed unto his house. And the LORD struck the child that Uriah's wife bare unto David, and it was very sick.

David therefore besought God for the child; and David fasted, and went in, and lay all night upon the earth.

And the elders of his house arose, and went to him, to raise him up from the earth: but he would not, neither did he eat bread with them.

And it came to pass on the seventh day, that the child died. And the servants of David feared to tell him that the child was dead: for they said, Behold, while the child was yet alive, we spake unto him, and he would not hearken unto our voice: how will he then vex himself, if we tell him that the child is dead?

But when David saw that his servants whispered, David perceived that the child was dead: therefore David said unto his servants, Is the child dead? And they said, He is dead.

Then David arose from the earth, and washed, and anointed himself, and changed his apparel, and came into the house of the LORD, and worshipped: then he came to his own house; and when he required, they set bread before him, and he did eat.

Then said his servants unto him, What thing is this that thou hast done? thou didst fast and weep for the child, while it was alive; but when the child was dead, thou didst rise and eat bread.

And he said, While the child was yet alive, I fasted and wept: for I said, Who can tell whether GOD will be gracious to me, that the child may live?

But now he is dead, wherefore should I fast? can I bring him back again? I shall go to him, but he shall not return to me. (2 Samuel 12:13-23)

Let's look at verses 13 and 14 in more detail. In verse 13 it says:

And David said unto Nathan, I have sinned against the LORD. (2 Samuel 12:13)

Notice that the sin here was David's sin. He personally had sinned. David had committed adultery with Bathsheba. She fell pregnant and David had her husband Uriah killed. He married Bathsheba and she gave birth to a son. David was guilty of not only adultery but also murder. Confronted by the prophet Nathan, David confessed his sin and Nathan replied:

The LORD also hath put away thy sin; thou shalt not die. (2 Samuel 12:13)

What a great comfort to David. He was the one who had sinned. He was worthy of early death and God in his mercy and grace said, "You're not going to die." We know that in Psalm 51 David confessed his sin and asked for forgiveness and so the mercy and grace of God prevailed. But we learn of something a little bit more perplexing in the next verse:

Howbeit, because by this deed thou hast given great occasion to the enemies of the LORD to blaspheme, the child also that is born unto thee shall surely die. (2 Samuel 12:14)

And someone cries, "Unfair!" Someone cries out, "What a cruel God!" Someone cries, "Why did the child die when it was the father who sinned?"

Those are valid questions. There are many things in life that are hard for us to understand and there are some things that God allows that we find difficult to comprehend. There are some important things we can learn from this, particularly in relation to sin and how our sin may affect others. Personal sin bears personal responsibility and personal accountability. In Ezekiel chapter 18 the bible states:

> **What mean ye, that ye use this proverb concerning the land of Israel, saying, The fathers have eaten sour grapes, and the children's teeth are set on edge? (Ezekiel 18:2)**

There was a proverb that was going around concerning whose fault it is that we are being judged for sin. Is it ours or can we blame our parents? We live in a generation and in a world that wants to place the blame for our sin on someone else. This goes all the way back to the Garden of Eden and Adam, Eve and the serpent.

That is the context of Ezekiel 18... Whose fault, is it? Why did this person die? Who is to blame for the death? When a death occurs, we want to know why did it happen? What was the cause of death? We are familiar with that nowadays with the pandemic. What do they write down as the cause of death? According to the Bible, the root cause of death is sin:

> **The soul that sinneth, it shall die. (Ezekiel 18:20)**

Immediately a question pops into your head, well, please tell me why David didn't die, and the child did? It seems unfair. And people are prone to call out unfair to God when they don't know and understand what God was doing or why. This verse continues:

> **The son shall not bear the iniquity of the father, neither shall the father bear the iniquity of the son: the righteousness of the righteous shall be upon him, and the wickedness of the wicked shall be upon him. (Ezekiel 18:20)**

People love to try and point out what they think are contradictions in the Bible. In Ezekiel, it says, the soul that sinneth it shall die and the son is not going to die for the sins of the father. And then we come to portions of scripture, such as in Exodus 34 and we find this passage mentioned several times:

> **Keeping mercy for thousands, forgiving iniquity and transgression and sin, and that will by no means clear the guilty; visiting the iniquity of the fathers upon the children, and upon the children's children, unto the third and to the fourth generation. (Exodus 34:7)**

The question remains, why was it that David lived, and the son died if each one of us is accountable for our own sin? What is this matter of bearing the iniquity of the fathers unto the third or fourth generation if we are personally accountable before God? How does that apply to David? How does that apply to his son who died?

Consider the matter of Job, who was one of the most righteous men of the day, the Bible tells us. Job lost about everything, and all his children died. Why did God allow that to happen? You cannot explain that other than to realize that Satan was at work behind the scenes.

I'm reminded also of this; scripture tells us that "it is appointed unto men once to die" (Hebrews 9:27). That is an interesting phrase. I want you to think outside of the box with me for just a moment. If it's appointed unto man once to die, why does the Bible speak of two deaths? The book of Revelation talks of those who face the second death. If it's appointed unto a man once to die, what is the second death?

The second death is damnation. It is described using the word perish. It refers to all who are lost and who will enter eternity condemned to the lake of fire, having rejected Jesus Christ as saviour. This is the final judgment, the second death which comes as payment for sin. I remind you that when it comes specifically to children, we read in Matthew chapter 18 God is not willing that any of these little ones should perish. It is not his will that these little ones spend eternity in the lake of fire. It is not his will that "any should perish, but that all should come to repentance" (2 Peter 3:9).

Do you think that when God created mankind it was his desire that man would sin and must be punished and die? Absolutely not. And many spend much of their time trying to figure out how God did something wrong along the way. He did nothing wrong along the way. I will repeat this, it was a man who sinned against God, not God who sinned against man. In fact, God in his mercy prepared a plan for all who would sin, it was and is through Jesus Christ who came into the world to save sinners. We forget what kind of a God we have.

There is a saying that I heard while in Bible college early on, which has stayed with me over the years. You may have heard it before, "one birth, two deaths; two births, one death."

When Jesus said to Nicodemus, you must be born again, Nicodemus thought, well I've already been born, what is he talking about "two births"? Jesus was talking about how every child of God is born physically into this world and then soon comes to realize that he is a sinner not only by nature but that he is also a sinner by choice. He realizes that if he does not do something about that as in having his sin forgiven and coming to know the Lord Jesus Christ as his saviour and experiencing a new birth, he will face two deaths otherwise known as the second death. He will face physical death which is the first death. And then he will face the spiritual death, which is the second death. This second death is eternal, with no second chance. There is no turning back from it, no changing it, no hope.

Why are we surprised when death occurs? When do we understand that every one of us apart from the rapture will face death? What really grips us more than the death of an adult is the death of an innocent little child, never knowing the Lord Jesus Christ as a saviour, never even knowing who the Lord Jesus Christ is, never knowing about God, never knowing what sin is.

Some of the most tough questions that I must try and answer always start with the word why. If we are going to talk about why and we are going to talk about God, I am not going to be able to give you an answer. His ways are higher than mine and his thoughts are higher than my thoughts. His ways are higher than yours and his thoughts are higher than your thoughts. (Isaiah 55:9) But when faced with unanswerable questions, we can and must fall back onto the revealed and certain truths of God which we know. We always know that in all circumstances, God is **"good and ready to forgive; and plenteous in mercy unto all them that call upon thee" (Psalm 86:5). We know that "his work is perfect: for all his was are judgment: a God of truth and without iniquity, just and right is he" (Deuteronomy 32:4).**

David had an expectation. God had already told David what was going to happen. God had sent the prophet Nathan to tell David that his sin had been put away. But the problem comes back in understanding verse 14 where it says:

> **Howbeit, because by this deed thou hast given great occasion to the enemies of the LORD to blaspheme, the child also that is born unto thee shall surely die. (2 Samuel 12:14)**

So, you are David, and you are thinking, all right, God has already told me what is going to happen. My child is at some stage going to die. David was not told when it would happen. Then the Lord struck the child that Uriah's wife bares unto David, and it was sick. In David's mind, he was no doubt thinking, this is it. What parent would not pray for the child? What parent would not weep, fast, and pray? Especially if you're a child of God and know that God can heal and answers prayer and just maybe, he will change his mind. Have you ever prayed like that? I know what God said and I know what the doctor said but maybe God will change his mind. Expectations. I would say to you that in the heart of David there was a hope and an expectation that something could be done. We look at it verse 15 which states:

> And Nathan departed unto his house. And the LORD struck the child that Uriah's wife bare unto David, and it was very sick.
>
> David therefore besought God for the child; and David fasted, and went in, and lay all night upon the earth.
>
> And the elders of his house arose, and went to him, to raise him up from the earth: but he would not, neither did he eat bread with them. (2 Samuel 12:15-17)

David, therefore, besought God for the child. Can you imagine the guilt of David as he realizes that it is his sin that is hurting his child? Well, that's heartbreaking, is it not? David goes and prays and weeps and fasts and the Bible tells us that he went in and lay all night upon the earth. The elders came in as they were concerned for him, and they tried to get him to eat. In verse 18 we read:

> And it came to pass on the seventh day, that the child died. And the servants of David feared to tell him that the child was dead: for they said, Behold, while the child was yet alive, we spake unto him, and he would not hearken unto our voice: how will he then vex himself, if we tell him that the child is dead? (2 Samuel 12:18)

I would submit to you that David had an expectation and a hope that when he prayed this would not be the time. He was praying that God would do something. My advice to you is that when you have somebody that is sick and you are concerned, do not stop praying. Because you never know what God might do. Here's David's expectation. He believed in God and trusted in God. His expectation was that through his praying and fasting the child would live. Well, the expectation on David's part at that point in time did not happen. God had already told him what would happen to the child, just not when it would happen.

Over the course of years in the ministry, I have tried to counsel people whose loved ones were laying on their death beds and they would say, "I know that God is going to heal them." I would come away appreciating the fact that they were going to trust God. But I did not tell them how it bothered me that they might be in for a great disappointment. It breaks my heart because you do not want to bring any disappointment or take away from someone's faith. God can heal. God can do anything. He is a miracle-working God. We just do not know if he will heal. Here we find David fasting and praying because he knows God's grace and great power to heal and deliver. He believes God can, but he'd have been wrong to say God absolutely would. Particularly already knowing that God had said that the child was going to die. Now notice what happened a little bit further if you would:

And it came to pass on the seventh day, that the child died. And the servants of David feared to tell him that the child was dead: (2 Samuel 12:18)

They have seen him weeping and praying and not wanting to eat and they're thinking, my, if that's what he did when the child was alive and sick, what's he going to do when the child dies? We do not really know what to say to people sometimes when somebody dies. These servants are so afraid to go tell David what has happened:

> But when David saw that his servants whispered, David perceived that the child was dead: therefore David said unto his servants, Is the child dead? And they said, He is dead. (2 Samuel 12:19)

David experienced a great disappointment. Life is not going the way he planned. His innocent baby boy has died because he foolishly, selfishly sinned. It seems unfair and David could have been angry and bitter but wait a minute, read on:

> Then David arose from the earth, and washed, and anointed himself, and changed his apparel, and came into the house of the LORD, and worshipped: then he came to his own house; and when he required, they set bread before him, and he did eat. (2 Samuel 12:20)

David gets up, washes get changed. He no longer weeps, and he no longer prays. Why no more weeping? You see, one of the facts of scripture that we learn from this passage is that David understood that after the child is dead, no prayer is going to bring him back. This cuts through the false doctrine that you can pray for the dead. You cannot. It is too late. David understood that.

David was a man of God. David was a man who trusted in God. David had failed God. God had not failed David. David knew that and came to some realizations. When a little one dies, there is hope. We do not have to sorrow as those who have no hope. But there is a qualification, as an adult, you only have that hope if you know the Lord. My, that should cause us to tremble sometimes as parents and that should cause us to tremble as individuals when we stop and consider that this hope is qualified. David explained his confusing behaviour to those who were watching him:

> Then said his servants unto him, What thing is this that thou hast done? thou didst fast and weep for the child, while it was alive; but when the child was dead, thou didst rise and eat bread.
>
> And he said, While the child was yet alive, I fasted and wept: for I said, Who can tell whether GOD will be gracious to me, that the child may live? (2 Samuel 12:21-22)

In the time of your expectations, while there is still life and there is still breath, continue to weep and to pray. Fast and go before the Lord because you and I are not God. We do not know what God is going to do in any given circumstance. We may know what the authorities tell us, what the doctors tell us, and what everyone else thinks, but we are not God. Do not give up hope. Continue in prayer but when the child or loved one dies, the time for prayer for that person is over. Look at David's reply:

> But now he is dead, wherefore should I fast? can I bring him back again? I shall go to him, but he shall not return to me. (2 Samuel 12:23)

David had sinned not the son. Why was it that the child died and not David? Why is it that God has promised that the sins of the father shall be visited unto the third and fourth generation? How does all that fit together? Remembering that God had said that this was going to be a shame to the nation of Israel. Can you imagine if that child had lived? They would always have been pointing the finger at that child. We know how you came about. He would be a shame to the nation of Israel, and he would have been a constant reminder to David of his shame.

I would submit to you, that what we understand from scripture here, David was guilty, and the son was innocent. David would face death but not the second death because he was forgiven. The son would face death but not the second death because he was innocent. He had no guilt of his own and he was innocent of the guilt of the father. What happened to the child was an indirect consequence of the sin of the father, not a direct consequence of the sin of the child. We must understand that. The child died and David said that he would go to see him again.

If you look back and study the life of David and what God said about David and his children and his sons, it is never quoted anywhere in scripture that he would see Absalom again. Absalom had openly rebelled against God. Absalom was of an age that he had sinned against God and sinned against his father openly and knowingly. I find it interesting that when it comes to this innocent child, David had the confidence that he would see his little one again. But when it came to the matter of Absalom and his death, David grieved over the death of Absalom without speaking of any hope of seeing him again.

That should wake up every child of God to realize that we might have relatives who are living a life apart from God who have yet to come to an understanding of their need for salvation while there is still hope. Barring the rapture, death will visit every family. Maybe death has already visited your family and it will visit other families. The only question is, what will the outcome be in eternity? **"For as in Adam all die, even so in Christ shall all be made alive"** (**1 Corinthians 15:22**).

I want to point out the responsibility you and I as adults and as parents have. Our obedience can bring great blessings to future generations, but our disobedience can have a negative effect on the third and the fourth generation. This is one of those portions of scripture that early on I found so hard to understand and comprehend. What does it mean that the children will bear the iniquity of the father to the third and to the fourth generation? If you grow up as a child in a household where the father and the mother are drunks and drug addicts, it is going to influence you. It will have a negative effect. You may not have much food to eat, and the bills may not be paid. You might have to run around without the right amount of clothes because of the sins of the father. It was not because you did anything wrong. It was because of the sins of the father.

If you live in a Christian household where the parents refuse to live by faith and refuse to step out in faith and obey God in faith, the sins of the father will be felt to the next generations. These consequences might be the absence of blessings that could have been given. God may not give them those victories which he could have given, and this will influence the children unto the third and the fourth generation to miss blessings they might have had. This too is a very sobering thought.

The spies who went to visit the promised land saw that it was just as God had promised. They saw the fruit and the fertile, flourishing fields, the walled cities, and well-watered plains. But they feared. They did not obey God in faith. Because of their unbelief, they failed to go in. Consequently, they died in the wilderness due to a lack of faith in trusting God. What is the warning? The warning is this, while you and I can talk about our own personal sin, and that our child will not die because of our sin, our sin can have a negative effect upon our children and their wellbeing in life up unto the third and the fourth generation. Think about it.

When we think about parents who have lost an infant child, we need to be careful in our response if those parents are lost. We can provide them with hope through the scripture that if they come to know the Lord Jesus Christ as saviour, there is a promise that they will meet again. You and I as a child of God have confidence that we will see our little ones again. I look forward to heaven to see the Lord Jesus Christ first and then to see Dawn Joy whom I never got to meet face to face here.

I would remind you of the warning. What happened to David can happen to you or me, young or old. There is a consequence for sin. Sin has a price tag on it. Young people, sin has a price tag on it. Adults, sin has a price tag on it. You can justify yourself by thinking that it will only affect you, but the truth is, that our sin always and inescapably influences others. The Bible says,

"Be not deceived; for God is not mocked: for whatsoever a man soweth, that shall he also reap" (Galatians 6:7).

Let us then take both the warning and the comfort of scripture and be encouraged. Know that God is "**gracious and merciful, slow to anger, and of great kindness**" (Joel 2:13). Our little ones will not perish. They are forever safe. And though our sins "**be as scarlet, they shall be as white as snow; though they be red like crimson, they shall be as wool**" (Isaiah 1:18). Sins may be visited to the third and fourth generation, but he "**keepeth covenant and mercy with them that love him and keep his commandments to a *thousand* generations**" (Deuteronomy 7:9).

One final thought in the death of David's son might be this; Paul said to live is Christ and to die is gain. While we may grieve, the loss is understandable; the child who is in heaven will never have to face the evils and disappointments of this life, in a sense, it is gain for them, not loss.

CHAPTER FIVE
AGE OF INNOCENCE

But of the tree of the knowledge of good and evil,
thou shalt not eat of it: for in the day that thou eatest
thereof thou shalt surely die.

(Genesis 2:17)

What does it mean to have no knowledge of good and evil? There was a time when Adam and Eve had no knowledge of good and evil. It is called the age of innocence. There is also a time in every person's life when they are without the knowledge of good and evil. They are innocent before God. We read in Deuteronomy:

> But Joshua the son of Nun, which standeth before thee, he shall go in thither: encourage him: for he shall cause Israel to inherit it.
>
> Moreover your little ones, which ye said should be a prey, and your children, which in that day had no knowledge between good and evil, they shall go in thither, and unto them will I give it, and they shall possess it. (Deuteronomy 1:38-39)

Let's go all the way back to the book of Genesis. In your bible study, it's always good to go back to what is called the law of the first mention. Try to take that as your starting point and follow its leading throughout the rest of the word of God. In Genesis chapter 2 we read:

> And out of the ground made the LORD God to grow every tree that is pleasant to the sight, and good for food; the tree of life also in the midst of the garden, and the tree of knowledge of good and evil. (Genesis 2:9)

We continue in verse 17 which says:

> But of the tree of the knowledge of good and evil, thou shalt not eat of it: for in the day that thou eatest thereof thou shalt surely die. (Genesis 2:17)

These are the instructions given by God to Adam and Eve. We know that Satan always tries to undermine, soften, weaken or change the word of God. In chapter 3, he comes to challenge Eve and deceive her. Notice what he said:

> For God doth know that in the day ye eat thereof, then your eyes shall be opened, and ye shall be as gods, knowing good and evil. (Genesis 3:5)

That was the challenge that Satan laid before Eve. He said that God was keeping the tree of the knowledge of good and evil from them, because if they ate of it, they wouldn't die, but would in fact be enlightened and become like God.

We jump down now to verse 22, which tells us:

> And the LORD God said, Behold, the man is become as one of us, to know good and evil: and now, lest he put forth

his hand, and take also of the tree of life, and eat, and live for ever:

Therefore the LORD God sent him forth from the garden of Eden, to till the ground from whence he was taken. (Genesis 3:22-23)

Now I'd like for you to look at Hebrews chapter 5:

For every one that useth milk is unskilful in the word of righteousness: for he is a babe.

But strong meat belongeth to them that are of full age, even those who by reason of use have their senses exercised to discern both good and evil. (Hebrews 5:13-14)

The idea of full age here is one who is an adult in terms of understanding. A distinction is being made between the knowledge of an infant and the knowledge of one who is an adult. The standpoint is that the child is not able to discern the difference between good and evil, but adults are.

Adam and Eve did not have a knowledge of good and evil when created. We must understand that principle. There was a time when Adam and Eve didn't know what was good and they didn't know what was evil. We could put it this way. They had it good and didn't really know it. It was the age of innocence. On each day of creation, God declared that "**it was good.**" God knew that it was good. Adam and Eve didn't know whether it was good or evil, or how to contrast one from the other.

Can you imagine a world where there was only good? We cannot fathom that. Adam and Eve lived there for a while. We know all about a world with evil. We truly do live in an evil world. Can you imagine a world where there is no death, no evil and no sorrow? The only time that is going to happen is in eternity for the child of God. Scripture makes it clear that these children are innocent and thus FOREVER SAFE.

Prior to the fall, Adam and Eve had obeyed God's command. They had not sinned. They only knew good and they did not know what it means to sin by experience. They knew that it was good, but they did not know just how good they had it until they lost it. God was fair in giving instructions. So, you cannot as many do, try to blame God. God told them that in the day that they partook of the fruit of the tree of the knowledge of good and evil, they would surely die. The sad news is, that they did partake of the tree. And the sad news is, they died. Their physical death was not immediate, but their spiritual death was. We understand that there are two types of death in the Bible. There is physical death and there is spiritual death. Revelation tells us that the second death, the spiritual death is eternal damnation in the lake of fire to all those without Christ who have died in their sins.

The key factor was the obedience to not eating the fruit of the tree of knowledge of good and evil. Satan challenged them on that and Adam and Eve both partook of the tree. They disobeyed God. God who is true and cannot lie, had to be true to His word. And at that point, the age of innocence was over. All of creation was affected by that decision (Genesis 3:17-19, Romans 8:22).

What I find interesting is this. Of all the trees in the garden, two are specifically mentioned. One was the tree of life. The other was the tree of the knowledge of good and evil. Adam and Eve were told that they could eat of any tree of the garden including the tree of life. Did they understand what that meant? Not necessarily. They were free to partake of any tree and the tree of life was included. What happened was just after they sinned, they were driven out of the garden, and they were no longer able to partake of the tree of life. You do not find this mentioned again until the book of Revelation where it speaks of the tree of life. They forfeited their right to eternal life when they partook of the tree of the knowledge of good and evil in disobedience to God and the age of innocence was over.

What does all this mean? It comes back to this one thread that we want to consider, the knowledge of good and evil. I would like to submit to you that they had an intellectual knowledge of what would happen with that tree if they were to partake because God had warned them. They knew that if they ate of this tree they would surely die. They knew it intellectually. But they did not know it by experience. When Satan tempted them and challenged them and they fell prey to that, they sinned, and they then knew it by experience. It is one thing to know sin by knowledge, it is another thing to know sin by experience.

It is therefore important in our discussion to understand that this truth applies to little children. Even though a child is born with a sin nature, you can explain to him all you want about what sin is, but until he sins by experience, he will not know what sin is. A parent can tell a child, do not do this, do not do that, do not touch the stove. The child will know it is hot by the intellect but until he touches it, he will he not really understand what hot is. There is a difference between intellectual knowledge and experiential knowledge.

One of the things which happened when Adam and Eve sinned comes back to what we call federal headship. When Adam sinned, the sin nature was passed down from him to all future generations. That is why the Bible says, **"as in Adam all die"** (1 Corinthians 15:22). Every child is now born with a sin nature but not every child born with a sin nature has sinned by experience. Little ones do not even know the difference between good and evil. That my friend is the key. They know nothing of guilt caused by sin.

What happened to Adam and Eve after they sinned? We find that they hid from God. There was no guilt beforehand. There was no need of the conscience to convict them of their sin. They had an innocent conscience but after they sinned, they had a defiled conscience. A defiled conscience carries with it the aspect of conviction and guilt due to sin.

They now know what is good and what is evil through experience. Some people put it this way. You never know what good is until you have lost it. You never know how good you have it until its gone. Adam and Eve suddenly began to realize what they had lost due to their disobedience to God. Their eyes were opened so that they could see things they never knew before and never needed to know before. If they had simply depended upon God rather than following their desire to have and to know, they would not have failed. It is due to this principle of federal headship that the Bible says:

> For *all* have sinned, and come short of the glory of God; (Romans 3:23)

In Isaiah we read:

> Butter and honey shall he eat, that he may know to refuse the evil, and choose the good.
> For before the child shall know to refuse the evil, and choose the good, the land that thou abhorrest shall be forsaken of both her kings. (Isaiah 7:15-16)

I want you to notice a statement that is made here, a principle, and that is that there is a time when a child does not even know to refuse the evil and choose the good because he does not yet know what is right and what is wrong. Salvation is a choice for you and I. Little ones do not understand God's law and they do not know how to refuse evil and choose the good. They are still innocent.

In Isaiah chapter 8 we read with regards to the age of innocence:

> And I went unto the prophetess; and she conceived, and bare a son. Then said the LORD to me, Call his name Mahershalalhashbaz.

For before the child shall have knowledge to cry, My father, and my mother. (Isaiah 8:3)

Think about that. How many times have you heard the first words out of the mouth of a child, and she utters mum, mum, mum but she is talking to the father? Or vice versa, dad, dad, dad and holds her arms out to the mother? The child is not able to distinguish between mother and father. We are clearly talking about one who does not know how to make the right choice here, does not even yet know the difference between a father and a mother and certainly doesn't know the difference between right and wrong or good and evil. These are the ones that Deuteronomy says will go into the promised land. They have not known sin experientially. They haven't gotten to that place yet where they have sinned and openly rebelled against a holy God and known it.

Now we understand the context of what is stated in Hebrews chapter 5. Certain believers should be acting like adults and be teaching others but they're not, they're still acting like babes. It tells us:

For every one that useth milk is unskilful. (Hebrews 5:13)

A babe is one whose stomach can only manage milk. You feed baby's milk; you do not feed them steak. We realize that understanding and personal responsibility help to define the biblical use of the word babe. Unskilful means ignorant of certain things, and inexperienced in certain areas. They do not yet know. They have not yet been taught. They have no idea.

In verse number 14 we see the contrast with maturity:

But strong meat belongeth to them that are of full age, even those who by reason of use have their senses exercised to discern both good and evil. (Hebrews 5:14)

This is referring to an adult who should now know, who should now have practice and experience. It was interesting to study the use of the word "**senses**". We know how important the five senses are so that we might relate to the world. Senses have to do with perception. I can smell something good, or I can smell something bad. I can taste something good, or I can taste something bad. Information about our world is sent from the senses immediately to the brain and this information informs our judgment and response. I hear something and I either jump or if you are deaf, you ignore it altogether.

In a spiritual context the unbeliever is described as sensual (Jude 19). He has no concept of who God is. He has no spiritual knowledge or discernment. Does that little child, that one-year-old, that two-year-old understand the knowledge of good and evil? Does he know how to discern both good and evil? Does he understand who God is and how he must obey him? No, he does not. Little ones are innocent of guilt. They are ignorant of God's law, and they are inexperienced in the matter of sin. They have no knowledge of good and evil. They are FOREVER SAFE and by God's grace will never perish when not knowing good or evil.

CHAPTER SIX

A GUILTY CONSCIENCE

And herein do I exercise myself, to have always a conscience
void of offence toward God, and toward men.

(Acts 24:16)

D eath is a separation. We don't know when any of us will pass into
eternity. We wonder if we will ever see our departed loved ones
again. For the child of God, there is great comfort from the scriptures that
we will meet again. This was a prevailing theme in the book of Job. Even
though Job was such a righteous man, he experienced great calamity and
sorrow and loss, even the loss of his children. He became very familiar
with death and asked many questions of the Lord concerning death. We
read in Job chapter 1:

> While he was yet speaking, there came also another, and
> said, Thy sons and thy daughters were eating and drinking
> wine in their eldest brother's house:
>
> And, behold, there came a great wind from the wilderness,
> and smote the four corners of the house, and it fell upon

the young men, and they are dead; and I only am escaped alone to tell thee. (Job 1:18-19)

What a tragic scene. He lost his children in a sudden, terrible disaster. Job asked the Lord why. Job's so-called three friends tried to help him out, but they ran into some difficulties trying to make sense of what had happened. In Job chapter 4 Eliphaz said this:

Remember, I pray thee, who ever perished, being innocent? (Job 4:7)

Eliphaz brought out the question, "You must be guilty. Whoever perished being innocent?" We've looked at the word innocent from the standpoint of being not guilty before a court of law. Then we come back to Job 14:14:

If a man die, shall he live again? all the days of my appointed time will I wait, till my *change* come. (Job 14:14)

I don't know about you but as a child of God, I'm looking forward to the rapture, not death. In any event, there's going to be a change that takes place.

In chapter 19 Job says:

For I know that my redeemer liveth, and that he shall stand at the latter day upon the earth: And though after my skin worms destroy this body, yet in my flesh shall I see God:

Whom I shall see for myself, and mine eyes shall behold, and not another; though my reins be consumed within me. (Job 19:25-27)

Job believed that he would live again in a resurrected body. Eliphaz was sure of only one thing; the innocent doesn't perish. Who is innocent? Is there anyone who is innocent? The only one who lived a life without sin was the Lord Jesus Christ. And yet, when we think of the little children, for how long do they remain innocent according to conscience, according to the knowledge of good and evil? How long? We would like to know the answers to these questions, we would like to know a particular age.

The Bible doesn't give us an age. Instead, it gives us the truth, that **"the wages of sin is death; but the gift of God is eternal life through Jesus Christ our Lord"** (Romans 6:23). It teaches us that **"all have sinned and have come short of the glory of God"** (Romans 3:23). When does one sin knowingly? When does a child transition from an innocent soul to a guilty sinner? When do children become sinners by choice and guilty before God?

I want to make this statement. You can take it as pure stewartology, (I do not know if there is any such thing as pure stewartology but merely consider it my own opinion) it is my thought the older I get the more I begin to wonder how many people are truly saved. That is a frightening statement. You see people who live a life in rebellion to God and never seem to be convicted, it makes you wonder. As we think about little children and their ability to understand the gospel and the age at which this understanding develops, we must question how many times a little child has been led in the sinner's prayer out of a parent's desire to see them saved rather than a personal conviction or independent choice of their own. I am a parent. Many of you are parents. Any godly parent would want their child to be saved, yet conviction of sin against God is a personal matter.

The danger is this. I am afraid that at times little children have been told to repeat a sinner's prayer and then told that they are saved. They go through all of life having never ever really come to godly repentance unto salvation. They may have been deceived by the devil himself. I do not know about you but that increasingly concerns me the longer I live. When I see children brought up in Christian homes and later turn away from

God, it makes me wonder, did they ever really come to know that they are a sinner before God? Did they ever really understand and know what sin is? Did they ever have a time of true repentance?

In the ministry, I have had many times when parents have brought their children to me to get saved. Well, yes, they need to be saved but I scratch my head and say, "Why don't you lead them to the Lord?" I do not have any special power over them. I can appreciate their concern but there is no need for you to get saved if you have never been lost. Jesus said it very well. He said, **"they that are whole need not a physician; but they that are sick"** (Luke 5:31).

We need to be careful about trying to get people saved who have never understood what it means to sin against God, never understood what it means to be lost, because then there is no need of repentance. And without repentance there is no salvation. We want children to get saved but we certainly do not want them to be deceived into a false sense of salvation, a salvation that has seen no repentance and where they have never understood what sin is.

We need to make sure that it's not just a matter of believing in Jesus Christ but believing on the work of the Lord Jesus Christ. Why are you going to believe on the Lord Jesus Christ? Because you come to realize that you're a sinner and that the wages of sin is death but the gift of God is eternal life through Jesus Christ our Lord.

I'm not saying to you, don't be concerned about your little children. I'm not saying that at all. I'm not saying that you should turn them away. But I am saying you can't make the decision for them. And so, there's a caution with all of this because we want to make sure that they are truly born again. But what about those who have never come to know sin? Look with me at John chapter 8:

They say unto him, Master, this woman was taken in adultery, in the very act. (John 8:4)

We know according to scripture that was a sin. The Pharisees knew that according to the law. They brought her to the Lord and said:

Now Moses in the law commanded us, that such should be stoned: but what sayest thou? (John 8:5)

You might circle that word *law* because that's going to be very important for where we're going with this. The law said that if you've committed adultery, the penalty was death. John tells us they were not interested in justice but in entrapment:

This they said, tempting him, that they might have to accuse him. But Jesus stooped down, and with his finger wrote on the ground, as though he heard them not.

So when they continued asking him, he lifted up himself, and said unto them, He that is without sin among you, let him first cast a stone at her. (John 8:6-7)

I wonder who that might be. I wonder if there's anybody like that. Jesus knew the answer to that question. And I'm sure they knew the answer to that question too. Notice what he says, **"He that is without sin among you, let him first cast a stone at her."**

Now here's what I want you to notice:

And they which heard it, being convicted by their own conscience, (John 8:9)

"Being convicted by their own conscience", that's the phrase, my friend, that I want us to consider. Those who knew what the law said, who knew that the transgression of that law meant death, brought her to the Lord Jesus Christ to test him. When he looked back at her and said that he who was without sin should be the first one to cast a stone, the Bible tells us that they were convicted by their own conscience. At what point is a 2-year-old convicted by his own conscience? At what point is a 1-year-old convicted by his own conscience?

What exactly is a conscience? Webster's 1828 dictionary says that it's an internal knowledge or moral sense which enables us to judge the difference between right and wrong. It is an inner moral compass "which decides on the lawfulness or unlawfulness of our actions and affections, and instantly approves or condemns them."

Vines expository dictionary puts it this way, it says that conscience is "that faculty by which we apprehend the will of God, as that which is designed to govern our lives." What 2-year-old or infant who doesn't even know that God exists, has a clear conscience of right and wrong? Do we not spend time teaching a child what is right and what is wrong because they do not know? They do not have the knowledge of good and evil. And they are not convicted of it. We can look at it in that sense because their conscience is not developed to understand that. They simply do not yet know or understand.

Turn with me to Romans chapter 2 and look at what the apostle Paul said under the inspiration of the Holy Spirit of God, Paul who knew what it was to be a sinner, Paul who knew what it was to be saved. He states:

> **Which shew the work of the law written in their hearts, their conscience also bearing witness, and their thoughts the mean while accusing or else excusing one another. (Romans 2:15)**

When is the work of the law written in our hearts? We all have a conscience, but little ones, whose conscience is not yet developed, may not be able to discern what is right and what is wrong. I know what I want

61

but what does God want? I know what my parents want and know what they have said, but what about the will of God? They begin to learn what is right and what is wrong. They do not automatically know this. In fact, the Bible is referred to as our schoolmaster. Show me the child which automatically knows what is right and what is wrong? You will not find one. Other than the Lord Jesus Christ.

Have you ever quoted somebody the word of God and they say, "Well, I'm not convicted by that"? Or have you told somebody that what they are doing is wrong and they say, "I'm not convicted"? What happens when you show them the word of God? The Holy Spirit is indeed working to convict them, whether they acknowledge it or not. Turn with me to 1 Corinthians chapter 8:

> **Howbeit there is not in every man that knowledge: for some with conscience of the idol unto this hour eat it as a thing offered unto an idol; and their conscience being weak is defiled. (1 Corinthians 8:7)**

Have you ever wondered why some people understand what sin is and other people do not? It goes back to the matter that some have a very weak conscience, and these things just do not make any difference to them. We read further in verse 10:

> **For if any man see thee which hast knowledge sit at meat in the idol's temple, shall not the conscience of him which is weak be emboldened to eat those things which are offered to idols; (1 Corinthians 8:10)**

People see, people, do. We are living epistles known and read of all men (2 Corinthians 3:2). Some may never have heard the word of God or read the word of God but the difference between what you do and what they do will be enough to bring them to a conviction of their sin.

Have you ever had anybody ask you why you do or do not do something? Why do they ask? Their conscience is convicting them. That is why it is so important for us to be living epistles known and read of all men, **"written not with ink, but with the Spirit of the living God; not in tables of stone, but in fleshy tables of the heart"** (2 Corinthians 3:3).

The Bible says some have a weak conscience:

> **But when ye sin so against the brethren, and wound their weak conscience, (1 Corinthians 8:12)**

What is the difference between a weak conscience and a defiled one? What kind of conscience does a newborn infant have? Or a little child? Is it a defiled conscience? Is it a conscience that automatically knows who God is? A conscience that knows that they are responsible before God? I would say to you no. Oh yes, they have a sin nature and whenever that sin nature is awakened there is a problem. But until that point in time, they are not aware of God, of sin, or of righteousness. They have no understanding of repentance or salvation.

In Acts chapter 23 the apostle Paul said:

> **And Paul, earnestly beholding the council, said, Men and brethren, I have lived in all good conscience before God until this day. (Acts 23:1)**

You and I as believers were at one time convicted of our sin. We knew that we were sinners. We realized that we were lost and undone and we understood that the Bible says, the wages of sin is death. The Holy Spirit of God convicted us, and we had that guilt that was within, and we knew that we needed to be saved. When we get saved God wipes our slate clean. We are declared righteous before him. We are justified, just as if we had never sinned. Our conscience is purified, guilt is removed and we become attentive to the Holy Spirit's conviction through the word of

God. Paul speaks of the matter of a good conscience before God. In Acts 24:16, he says, **"And herein do I exercise myself, to have always a conscience void of offence toward God."**

We could say that now a child is born and even before he is born, he has an undefiled conscience. He is a sinner by nature but not a sinner by knowledge and choice. It is when we become sinners that our pure conscience is defiled, our clear conscience is weakened, and we become guilty and ashamed. We are pricked in our conscience because we are condemned by our sin before the law of God.

Jesus was different. Hebrews chapter 7 tells us:

For such an high priest became us, who is holy, harmless, undefiled, separate from sinners, (Hebrews 7:26)

What was the difference? Jesus never sinned. He was undefiled. What it is to have defilement of conscience? The word defile means to smear with mud. To put a spot, a blemish there. Sin is a blemish. Sin defiles. When does that little child come to the point of realizing that they are guilty before God?

Let us look at what Paul wrote in Romans chapter 7:

What shall we say then? Is the law sin? God forbid. (Romans 7:7)

The law, my friend, is not the problem. But we think of it that way. Paul continues:

Nay, I had not known sin, but by the law: (Romans 7:7)

Look at those two words, *known sin.* When does that child know that they are a sinner? Now the law is not the problem. We live in a society that is constantly changing the laws to meet the demands and desires of sinful men. It changes laws so that man can sin with impunity. Sin is a transgression of the law of God no matter what the law of man may state. Paul continues:

> **for I had not known lust, except the law had said, Thou shalt not covet. (Romans 7:7)**

The little child takes a toy that belongs to somebody else, and the parent says, "Oh you should not do that. That is stealing." Oh, yes? Who said? The wise parents reply, "God said." The law teaches us what sin is. The problem is not the law. The problem is our own sinful hearts. Paul is pointing out the law, for he had not known lust, except the law had said, **Thou shalt not covet.**

> **But sin, taking occasion by the commandment, wrought in me all manner of concupiscence. (Romans 7:8)**

Remember, every child is born with a sin nature and given the time and opportunity will sin. They do not yet know it. How many parents understand this, that before a child can even say mother or father they somehow know how to cry out for their own way and their own will. Notice this in verse 9:

> **For I was alive without the law once: but when the commandment came, sin revived, and I died. (Romans 7:9)**

He said, For I was alive without the law. And when a child is born, they are very much alive without the law. They do not know what good is, they do not know what bad is. They do not know what evil is, they do not know what wrong is. They have not come to the standpoint that they have sinned openly and knowingly against the will of God. They are innocent. Innocent of guilt before God. That is why those little ones are safe, FOREVER SAFE. Because they are alive without the law.

What does it mean to revive? It means to wake up. At a certain point, every person will come to understand the difference between good and bad, their conscience convicting them when they sin and do wrong. Once he sins, he will want to do it repeatedly. He is awakened to sin and in need of salvation from the penalty and the power of sin.

Notice what he said, **"and I died" (Romans 7:9)**. That is such a powerful verse when you start to put it together. Adam and Eve knew that God said that if they were to partake of the tree of the knowledge of good and evil, they would surely die. They were alive in their communion with God. But the day they partook of that tree, they died. They died spiritually. There comes a point in time in the life of every child when they knowingly go and sin against God and they die spiritually. From that time forward they need to be saved. Up until that point in time, they are safe.

Was the law the problem? Paul was trying to explain that the law is not the problem. In fact, the law was a good thing. Notice what Paul said:

Wherefore the law is holy, and the commandment holy, and just, and good. (Romans 7:12)

Tell that to the man going down the road who knows that the speed limit says 70 but he is doing 90. The police officer stops him and says, "You're guilty." He replies, "Well I just don't like that law. I want to do 90 from hereon, and that law doesn't make any sense, it's not good for me." You can argue all you want, take it up with the judge, but you're still guilty. The law showed you your sin. That is why I say strongly that the children who have not come to that knowledge of good and evil are safe from the penalty of sin, until the point in time they come to know and understand, and their conscience is awakened, and sin revives, they die spiritually. In verse 13 we read:

Was then that which is good made death unto me? God forbid. (Romans 7:13)

Again, he said God forbid or perish the thought. You might be thinking, I wish God had never given us the law. No. Without that law, you were hopeless because you would never realize that you were a sinner and that you needed to be saved. It is the justice and mercy of God to give us the law to teach us of our sinfulness and of our need of a saviour. **"Wherefore the law was our schoolmaster to bring us unto Christ, that we might be justified by faith" (Galatians 3:24).** Jesus said plainly:

> **But when Jesus heard that, he said unto them, They that be whole need not a physician, but they that are sick. (Matthew 9:12)**

Jesus was making it clear that those who do not realize that they are lost, do not know that they need to be saved. And then he pointed out what was needed to be saved, which was repentance:

> **But go ye, and learn what meaneth, I will have mercy, and not sacrifice: for I am not come to call the righteous, but sinners to repentance. (Matthew 9:13)**

One of the tragedies of the day you and I live in is this easy believism, salvation without any kind of repentance. It is ruining lives and hurting churches. As parents, you need to make sure that your children understand what sin is, know that they are sinners and that they need to repent before God.

I am thankful to understand, that God has given you and I an assurance that up until that point in time, little ones are safe. Children that come up in the household of a family that loves the Lord and live for the Lord are going to come to that point of understanding much earlier than others. Whatever age it is, there must be an understanding of repentance. Without repentance, there is no salvation. You cannot get saved if you have never been lost. I am afraid that many who think they are saved, are in fact lost. Just because you said a few words in church and someone told you that you were saved, does not mean you are really saved. I am not trying to cast doubt on those who are truly born again. If there has never been a change of heart and a change of life, you need to re-examine yourself and ask, am I really saved? Does your life show it? The Bible says, **"Examine yourselves, whether ye be in the faith; prove your own selves" (2 Corinthians 13:5).**

I think as much as this topic of FOREVER SAFE is good and encouraging, it is also a warning. We need to understand what salvation is. We need to allow people, especially children, to come to a personal conviction from the word of God that they are indeed sinners and in need of a saviour.

God help us never to be deceived. Remember what the devil wanted to do. You'll not surely die, was his lie. He wants to confuse us. Thank God that Jesus said that he was not willing that any of these little ones should perish. If a man die, will he live again? Well, if he's a young child, he'll be safe. If he's older, he can be saved. The Bible talks about the lamb slain from the foundation of the world. God knew ahead of time what a free choice would do and what sin would do and so he provided hope through the Lord Jesus Christ.

CHAPTER SEVEN
COMFORT ONE ANOTHER

Wherefore comfort one another with these words.
(1 Thessalonians 3:2)

In 1 Corinthians 13, the apostle Paul said:

**When I was a child, I spake as a child, I understood as a
child, I thought as a child: but when I became a man, I put
away childish things.**

**For now, we see through a glass, darkly; but then face to
face: now I know in part; but then shall I know even as also
I am known. (1 Corinthians 13:12-13)**

Have you ever listened to the questions little children ask? They are
unique, very much straight to the point. I remember one day walking out of our house; I could not have been any more than five. I remember looking up at the dark sky and asking my mother and father who made the stars? That is a good question.

Questions can be good. When we are studying the Bible and asking a particular question, other side questions often come up with it. So it is when we think about FOREVER SAFE. When the question comes up concerning what happens to little children when they die, we find many other perplexing questions arise, which we might never have thought to ask otherwise.

In this chapter, I want to look at some of the extended questions which have been raised in this study. As we've gone along through this study, those often posed to me are examined here. We will look at them and try to answer them as best we can.

A question has been asked, what about those who die in miscarriage? I've long placed miscarriage and stillbirths into the same category, but as I have studied it in greater depth, I have learned that there is a distinction between them, although they share the same amount of grief.

Miscarriage is a term used for a pregnancy that ends before the 20th week of gestation. Stillbirths are when the baby dies in the uterus, most commonly after the 20th week. One question that many struggles to answer is when does life begin? I would say to you that according to scripture life begins at conception. Let us look at Psalm 139 where David spoke under the inspiration of the Holy Spirit, saying:

My substance was not hid from thee, when I was made in secret, and curiously wrought in the lowest parts of the earth.

Thine eyes did see my substance, yet being unperfect; and in thy book all my members were written, which in continuance were fashioned, when as yet there was none of them. (Psalm 139:15-16)

In other words, God had a plan, and God knew all about us before you and I ever knew anything about Him. Elizabeth's baby, the Bible tells us, **"leaped in her womb" (Luke 1:41)**. Life begins far earlier than when a child is born. We must understand and realize that the Bible shows us that children are **"an heritage of the LORD" (Psalm 127:3)**. As children are gifts from God to parents, we may understand that God cares for them and loves them even more than we do as parents. Therefore, whether it is a miscarriage, a stillbirth, or even an abortion, these unborn little ones are precious to him and thus FOREVER SAFE. If they die before knowing good and evil; they will be with the Lord in heaven, and that is a great comfort to parents in such times of loss and grief. Yes, there is hope.

The next question someone has asked is how does a child innocent of personal sin differ from an adult who has never heard the gospel? That's an age-old question that many of us have tried to answer. Many cry, "Unfair! Doesn't God care about those in heathen countries?" Are these adults the same as little ones in that they do not know the law of God nor understand the gospel?

There is a difference between little ones who are FOREVER SAFE and adults who have not heard the gospel yet in themselves have come to understand a sense of right and wrong. Read with me in Romans chapter 1:

> **For the wrath of God is revealed from heaven against all ungodliness and unrighteousness of men, who hold the truth in unrighteousness; Because that which may be known of God is manifest in them; for God hath shewed it unto them. (Romans 1:18-19)**

Wrath is the judgment of God. We've mentioned the fact that there's a distinction between the word perish, which speaks of judgment and the word sleep which is used to describe the death of saved people. The word perish is a reference to those who will face an eternal second death. Little children and infants will not perish. They will not meet the wrath of God. They do not know what sin is and they have not yet sinned knowingly. Notice that phrase, **"may be known of God"**. It is possible to know because God hath showed it unto them. How did he show it to them? Verse 20 answers that question:

> **For the invisible things of him from the creation of the world are clearly seen, being understood by the things that**

are made, even his eternal power and Godhead; so that they are without excuse: (Romans 1:20)

When we deal with the Godhead, we are also dealing with the nature of God and who he is. God has revealed himself through the creation of the world so that it can be clearly understood who he is. The Bible says, **"The heavens declare the glory of God. The firmament sheweth forth his handywork" (Psalm 19:1).** Creation reveals to all humanity that there is a creator. You and I know him as God, but not everybody understands or accepts that as a fact.

There is in everyone a moral conscience. The conscience of man is developed as we mature and understand between right and wrong, good and evil. In 2000 BC, there was the Code of Ur-Nammu; a civil code of right and wrong for society. Then there was the more well-known code of Hammurabi from 1750 BC. It was a collection of 282 rules establishing commercial and social laws and a justice system. These came before the giving of the law to Moses in 1450 BC. It demonstrates to us that there is a moral law written on peoples' hearts, as the Bible says:

For when the Gentiles, which have not the law, do by nature the things contained in the law, these, having not the law, are a law unto themselves:

Which shew the work of the law written in their hearts, their conscience also bearing witness, and their thoughts the mean while accusing or else excusing one another;) (Romans 2:14-15)

When Adam and Eve were created, they knew God, they spoke with God, and after they sinned, they hid from God because of a guilty conscience. Everything was good and perfect until they went against the known word of God. Then their eyes were opened, and they knew that they had sinned. All creation was marred by sin (Romans 8:22). Every person after that was born with a sin nature. Paul writes:

> **For as in Adam all die, even so in Christ shall all be made alive. (I Corinthians 15:22)**
>
> **The biblical responsibility for us as parents is to train our children and teach them to know**
>
> **and love and worship the Lord. We look in Judges, and it says:**
>
> **... and there arose another generation after them, which knew not the LORD, nor yet the works which he had done for Israel. (Judges 2:10)**

How does that happen? The Holy Spirit convicts the inner soul of man. He reveals God and makes Him known through creation and man's conscience. Thus, a man knows the need for these civil moral codes to teach right from wrong. Therefore, parents are to train their children in the knowledge of right from wrong.

You cannot place an infant who does not have any knowledge of good or evil in the same category as an adult. Though he may never have heard the gospel before, the adult is accountable to God for his response to God's witness in the creation and things clearly seen as stated in the book of Romans chapter one.

Another question which I want to cover is very intriguing. Will we recognize one another in heaven? May I caution you against sentimental, emotional answers? Sometimes I will be discussing something with someone, and they say, "Well, that just doesn't seem fair to me." We need our response to be biblically true, not what we'd like to be true. **"For now we see through a glass darkly, but then face to face" (I Corinthians 13:12).** I trust we can see that there are some things about heaven we will never know until we get there, that **"the secret things belong unto the**

LORD our God" (**Deuteronomy29:29**). We must acknowledge that God has not shown us and told us everything. I say that as a preface to the answer. Look with me now in Matthew chapter 18:

> **And I say unto you, That many shall come from the east and west, and shall sit down with Abraham, and Isaac, and Jacob, in the kingdom of heaven. (Matthew 8:11)**

I find that interesting because he names them specifically. On the mount of transfiguration, Peter, James and John saw Moses and Elijah and conversed back and forth with them. They were recognizable. The disciples were able to identify them as people, as Moses and Elijah. We will be able to identify Abraham, Isaac and Jacob in the kingdom of heaven. 1 Corinthians is known as the resurrection chapter. It tells us:

> **But some man will say, How are the dead raised up? and with what body do they come? (1 Corinthians 15:35)**

What will we look like in heaven? Will we recognize our loved ones? Paul continues:

> **It is sown a natural body; it is raised a spiritual body. (1 Corinthians 15:44)**

My body is decaying. Your body is deteriorating. You may not realize how much it is decaying. We are told that our resurrection body is a different kind of body. We cannot give details about that because we're not given a lot of detail from scripture. We know it is something different from what goes in the grave. We read further:

> **And as we have borne the image of the earthy, we shall also bear the image of the heavenly. (1 Corinthians 15:49)**

Who is that heavenly? It is the Lord Jesus Christ. Those who witnessed his resurrection give us some insight into the resurrection body, but the key is in verse 51:

> **Behold, I shew you a mystery; We shall not all sleep, but we shall all be changed, (1 Corinthians 15:51)**

Notice that he is speaking of saved people. He does not use the term die. He does not use the term death. He does not use the term perish. He talks about sleep because we will be waking up. The key is the word changed:

> **So when this corruptible shall have put on incorruption, and this mortal shall have put on immortality, then shall be brought to pass the saying that is written, Death is swallowed up in victory. (1 Corinthians 15:54)**

I know that in my new body, my resurrection body, I will not need glasses or hearing aids. No more weakness, no more pain. It will be a new body. What will it look like? The closest thing I can show to you is the resurrection body of the Lord Jesus Christ. John says:

> **We shall be like him; for we shall see him as he is. (1 John 3:2)**

Another tricky question is, what age will we be in heaven? This question is asked by those who have lost little ones in the womb. They think that their baby will forever be in its pre-birth state and size. I do not believe the Bible tells us exactly. But here is where I am going to step aside and say something of my own. While there is not a clear answer, the assumption based on scripture is that we will be of an ideal age, whatever that might be. Since there is recognition in heaven, it would be understood that the infants will no longer be infants but more of adult age. It is interesting to note that it was as adults that God created Adam and Eve.

For, behold, I create new heavens and a new earth: and the former shall not be remembered, nor come into mind.

But be ye glad and rejoice for ever in that which I create: for, behold, I create Jerusalem a rejoicing, and her people a joy.

And I will rejoice in Jerusalem, and joy in my people: and the voice of weeping shall be no more heard in her, nor the voice of crying.

There shall be no more thence an infant of days, nor an old man that hath not filled his days: for the child shall die an hundred years old; but the sinner being an hundred years old shall be accursed. (Isaiah 65:17-20)

This passage describes the millennial kingdom. Remember that in eternity time will be no more. We will not get any older; we will not get any younger. I would hate to think that I am still going to have an old, wrinkled body in eternity. We need to understand that it will be an ageless time. We will not age anymore. Does that mean that the unborn child will not be any older? Remember that it is a spiritual body, a glorified body. It is nothing like what we have now. It is a time of absolute perfection. There does not need to be any more development or improvement or growth.

It would help if you distinguished between the millennium and the eternal kingdom. There will be people who will be born and people who will die in the millennium. But the age factor will go back to how it was in the beginning of creation. The eternal kingdom will be an ageless time, and it will be a sinless time. It will be complete perfection. There will not be births or deaths in the eternal kingdom. There will not be marriages in the eternal kingdom. We will not be disappointed. We shall be like him, for we shall see him as he is.

The last question intrigued me. What about the rapture? Children and those still in the womb will all be taken in the rapture, along with those who are saved. What about the mother that is six months pregnant and unsaved? At the rapture, that mother will not have a baby anymore. What about the unbelieving mother holding a two-year-old little one in her arms? She will be grieving the sudden disappearance of her little child. Why? The child is not going to be judged but those who go into the tribulation period having rejected the Lord Jesus Christ will face a time of judgement as never seen before.

But I say unto you, That it shall be more tolerable for the land of Sodom in the day of judgment, than for thee. (Matthew 11:24)

Jesus is speaking about the judgment that is coming in the tribulation. This world is going to see sorrow as it has never seen before. I thank God that we understand that those little ones will not perish. **"Suffer little children, and forbid them not, to come unto me: for of such is the kingdom of heaven"** (Matthew 19:14).

My friend, thank God there is hope for grieving parents who know the Lord. Your little ones, as well as all who have never come to the knowledge of good and evil intellectually and who have departed this life, are with the Lord. It is abundantly clear through scripture that they have never known good or evil and as such are not facing a judgement for personal sin and are FOREVER SAFE. He also has made it clear that he is not willing that they should perish but are part of the kingdom. They have escaped the evils of this world that you and I now know. Wherefore as the scripture saith, **"Comfort one another with these words"**. It is my desire to provide you with a hope that is sure based on the hope provided and promised in the word of God.

They are FOREVER SAFE.

The most important question I would ask is what about you? If you do not know the Lord Jesus Christ, you will be forever separated from your little ones. Today is your opportunity. If you want to be reunited with that little one when you die, the only way possible is through the Lord Jesus Christ. Where will you spend eternity? Where will you be when the rapture takes place? Remember, the Lord is not willing that any should perish. You must repent of your sins calling on the Lord Jesus Christ today to forgive you and save you. He has promised, "For whosoever shall call upon the name of the Lord shall be saved" (Romans 10:13).

May God richly bless you and to those who have suffered the loss of one of these little ones, may God be your stay and comfort until you meet again.